MAR 0 2 '01   **DATE DUE**

GAYLORD			PRINTED IN U.S.A.

A Children's Book About

BEING FORGETFUL

Managing Editor: Ellen Klarberg
Copy Editor: Annette Gooch
Editorial Assistant: Lana Eberhard
Art Director: Jennifer Wiezel
Production Artist: Gail Miller
Illustration Designer: Bartholomew
Inking Artist: Micah Schwaberow
Coloring Artist: Linda Hanney
Lettering Artist: Linda Hanney
Typographer: Communication Graphics

Printed in 1991

A Children's Book About

BEING FORGETFUL

By Joy Berry

GROLIER ENTERPRISES CORP.

This book is about Lennie.

Reading about Lennie can help you understand and deal with **being forgetful.**

You are being forgetful when you do not remember something. When you forget something, you do not think about it.

Have you ever forgotten to do something?

Have you ever forgotten to tell someone something?

Have you ever forgotten to take something with you?

Have you ever forgotten and left something behind?

Forgetting something can frustrate you. It can frustrate others as well.

Try not to be forgetful.

There are things you can do to help yourself remember.

Do this to help you remember:

Ask yourself this question before you leave
someplace: "Am I forgetting anything?"

Do this to help you remember:

Ask someone to remind you about something you do not want to forget.

Do this to help you remember:

Write yourself a reminder. Pin the reminder to yourself, or put it in a place where you are sure to see it.

Do this to help you remember:

Write a reminder on the back of your hand with washable ink.

Do this to help you remember:

Put a string or adhesive tape around your finger. Be sure it is not too tight.

Do this to help you remember:

Put things you want to take with you in a special place so you will not forget them. A good place is next to the door so you will see them before you leave.

Being forgetful can be frustrating. You and the people around you will be happier if you do not forget things.